C000162037

GOD'S
SECRET

*Also by John Woolley
and published by Arthur James*

I Am With You

Sorrow Into Joy

Prayers for the Family

The Friendship of Jesus

Words of Power

GOD'S
SECRET

John Woolley

ARTHUR JAMES
JOHN HUNT PUBLISHING
NEW ALRESFORD
1999

First published in Great Britain in 1999 by

ARTHUR JAMES
an imprint of
JOHN HUNT PUBLISHING
46a West Street, New Alresford, Hants SO24 9AU
United Kingdom

The author would like to thank Fr. Gerald Vann and
Mr Peter Woolley for help in the preparation of this book.

John A. Woolley asserts the moral right
to be identified as the author of this work.

A catalogue record for this book is available
from the British Library.

ISBN 0 85305 448 7

Typeset in Adobe Goudy by
Strathmore Publishing Services, London N7

Printed and bound by
Tien Wah Press, Singapore

Contents

Introduction

There is a secret which God wishes to share!

Many have found the secret and it has revolutionized their way of living. *Without* the discovery, a Christian's life may not be as victorious as it is meant to be.

Here is a typical cry-from-the-heart. I wonder how many would identify with it?

> I do have occasional bursts of warm faith. I can appear joyful and very 'spiritual' at times. But I wonder how much I *really* have changed since I became a believer?

And could this be the desperate prayer which we may find ourselves saying?

> Lord, I am so busy on Your behalf; I say all the right things to others about knowing You and trusting You. I know

that I would be a much worse person without You … but I can't hide from You that there is so much darkness, so much sheer doubt, so many failure-areas …

There are lots of hurt places which still need Your healing. I can't go on excusing periods of coldness and doubt by saying that it's 'normal'.

Lord, You *must* know that I'm not a minute-by-minute Christian …

There's often a pressure upon Christians to present a 'joyful', 'victorious' image. I have met many who have done this for a while, refusing to admit to any doubts or difficulties, but then broken down – sometimes tearfully – in my presence.

That's why we must never be afraid to *confront* ourselves fearlessly, ready to admit that, inside, there is often a huge vacuum! If we want to learn God's secret, *realism* is always the best starting-place for learning it.

Chapter One

I wonder whether we could imagine our-selves, standing, completely alone, under the night sky?...

For a few moments, we have broken free from all our usual supports and friendships. We haven't got with us those well-loved books of devotion or even the memories of them. It is silent and chill. I wonder if the darkness is echoed, just a little, *inside us*?

Do we have, not so much a sense of God, but a sense of *longing*?

For some of us, in spite of our surface 'assurance', there may even have been moments of not wanting to go on living.

We may find those star-systems, glimpsed through the clouds, very attrac-tive, but so ... indifferent.

And God? Well, perhaps we thought that we had it all neatly tied down, but, as we stand here in the darkness, is there a feeling that God is only our own self-comforting invention?

Isn't the uncomfortable truth that we're absolutely alone?

And so, in the silence, we seem unable to rely on all the uplifting things which others have written. We remember, rather uncomfortably, how we have reassured other people with faith-filled phrases, which sounded a little hollow to ourselves!

Dare we trust any longer those warm faith-evocative occasions when we 'praised' God, along with other Christians? Dare we look at existence courageously – even if the conclusion could be the agnosticism which we have pitied in others?

Can what is all around us here in the darkness have any *possible* interest in us? Whatever has happened to the super-structure of faith and confidence which we thought we had acquired?

Does the pain of life which we observe every day, fit *best* into a universe which is dark and uncaring?

We linger for a little longer and, feeling empty, leave our little spot under the stars. Soon, though, we will return …

A few days later we find ourselves out under the stars once more. On that previous occasion, there was the strange feeling that the emptiness was, paradoxically, a somewhat mystical experience. But we're quite prepared, now, for another cold moment of truth'. Here, in the darkness, the old doubts come rushing back.

But it's not very long before there's a sense of something happening as part of this vacuum-experience. It's almost as if the darkness is trying to get through to us.

It's as if existence is *enfolding* us and making us feel very secure, even in the absence of tangible sources of security.

We daren't tear ourselves away, because it seems that something is being whispered into our hearts, ever so gently:

My child, this universe which you are pondering is *Myself* … *I* am expressed

in it. I share both the light and the
sadness of your life – and the lives of
all My children.

Suddenly, the darkness has become a
caring environment, as the heart-whisper
continues:

My child, I have made this creation the
setting in which you can find *true*
knowledge of Me ... The dark places
are the *very places* where you can make
the blinding discovery of My love ...

It is a love of which this universe is
merely one partial expression ...

This incredible universe is not so much
based on creative power, but an expression
of love! We're sure that we have come
across this description many times previously, but now, it fills our thoughts.

We're desperate to learn more, feeling
the sense of a secret about to be revealed.

Suddenly there is a strong feeling that
we have to give a name to the presence
enfolding us here in the darkness. A word

keeps intruding – a very familiar word, but this time causing us to feel a thrill.

The name which persists in coming to us is – 'Jesus'.

We begin to wonder how on earth people could ever regard that name as just the relatively narrow object of worship of one of the major world religions.

We find ourselves whispering the name with a sense of awe ... whispering it to ourselves – and to Him.

Our heart registers a response from the surrounding presence:

> Yes, this is My universe, and because of Me, God is now *knowable* for you.

After a moment or two, we have the strongest possible impression of some very familiar words – though they never sounded quite like this before:

> Come to Me ...

All at once, the daunting couldn't-care-less universe is eloquent and protective. This inescapable presence, under the night sky, *must* be the risen Saviour of our planet.

'Jesus' suddenly means Someone always existing – the place where love, suffering, doubt, the mysterious creation and the 'me' who has evolved through the centuries begin to come together and to make sense, at last.

Chapter Two

By now, there is no tearing oneself away from this encounter in the stillness. And soon, a further word is whispered into our heart:

> My child, there is so little *real* knowledge of Me …
>
> So many who claim to know Me are, in reality, missing the way …
>
> So many who eagerly seek Me are being *caused* to miss the way …
>
> Many subtle by-paths away from Me are not recognized for what they are …
>
> So many have become content with second-best, and feel that humanity cannot attain more in this life …
>
> Many have believed the lie that it is not possible really to know My presence consistently. And yet knowing Me is a gift which I have for *any* child of Mine.

When someone comes to know Me, that person may be mistrusted, or seen as deserving of pity.

So many cannot accept, fully, the truth revealed about Myself, and cannot accept My power to change lives.

Many who bear My name may be virtually blind about what, in the name of 'religion', can be pathetic hindrances to knowing Me …

Well! Here, under the night sky, we're not conscious of feeling cold or alone any more

There is now the even more persistent feeling that we're going to learn something crucial, a God-given secret, which will somehow change us.

Even now, we realize that we are not as confused as we used to be. We realize that something deeper than merely new insight is being given to us. There's a strong feeling that, when we go among people again, we'll never forget what is being shown to us. We feel that never again will we believe those who claim that it's impossible to say

I know'. We'll never again be content with that second-best.

Why didn't we realize, earlier, that God *wants* individuals to experience His protective and tenderly-loving nature? We see, vividly, that any branch of religion which does not uncompromisingly lead to this, is sadly lacking.

These thoughts are confirmed by another whisper into our heart:

> My child, I want you to come, as a pilgrim, on to the narrow way where My love *can* be found …
>
> So many hearts wish, desperately, to know that love …
>
> The most exciting journey you can make is to discover, in *this* life, the love of which I have spoken … the love which lies behind this creation …

The world continues to feel a more secure place for a few wonderful moments. But we must face the fact that, in a world like this, doubt is sure to re-assert itself. What can we do to *keep* the sense of 'I know'?

We now feel the need to be fully concentrated because we sense that God is about to reveal something important.

Then, as we give Him our full attention it gently comes:

> My child, I want you to see that My love for you is not just an attitude; it is an *influence*.

Chapter Three

So that's it. An *influence* …

Well! We have to admit that this seems a rather low-key divine secret! But this low-key secret is, in fact, a crucial one.

Here is God wanting us to know that He's not merely thinking of us lovingly, and occasionally intervening with a burst of power on our behalf. (Isn't that, honestly, what most of us feel?)

No. The truth being shown is a revolutionary one for us. God's love is, in fact, a change-bringing *influence* (there *all* the time), a conquering *influence*.

God's love is a *power* which reaches those deep places of the mind which are usually closed to us; it is something to affect every aspect of our existence. If we will let it!

Not an attitude, but an influence …

So many Christians wish, desperately, to feel God's love more warmly, or to know that they really have *changed* from the people they were. For such people, God offers the discovery of a wonderful way through. He wants us to be *receivers* of His love's influence – rather like being tuned in to a TV or radio signal – if that isn't too homely an illustration!

As we learn to recognize God's constant love-influence, our lives, which are intrinsically ones of change and uncertainty, acquire a marvellous stability. This is because the influence is *constant*.

But just a moment, what about the barriers? Yes, the barriers existing in that very complex me, the barriers of temperament and those results of what life has done to me. How can the love-influence get past these?

And so, we throw this question back at God: 'What about the barriers?' After a moment or two, we suddenly realize that God didn't 'ordain' these barriers in order to make knowing Him a near-impossible process. The barriers may have been erected from *our* side – not all intentionally, of course – the result of life-experiences, re-actions to pain, parental influences. But we now realize something else which is crucial about those barriers (and it's a wonderful realization): *God doesn't see them!*

Oh, but surely those barriers are real? The absence of love in my past, making it hard for me to relate, closely, to people (and to God, of course); the free-floating anxiety which attaches itself to almost everything; the sense of rejection; the sense of injustice, perhaps, about the way life has treated me, compared with others.

And then, there could be the barrier of a cold and barren existence left after the death of someone greatly loved. Surely, all of these are tremendous obstacles to know-ing God warmly and to enjoying His love?

But the message persists: God doesn't see these things as barriers against Himself. Painful areas (God would agree), but barriers? Emphatically, no.

Let us recognize those life-experiences, those temperament-limitations which we feel prevent us from experiencing God's love … Then, a deep breath, as we imaginatively allow God to look right *through* all those barriers – a look of love right into the very deepest part of us.

However 'hopeless' we may have felt our circumstances or our personal make-up to have been, we start to see that God's love now has the power to pierce our defences.

I cannot emphasize too strongly that *nothing* can stop His love reaching us, nor our *realizing* that love – simply because that love is a conquering influence. Our supposed barriers can be cut down to size, at last.

And so, in the best tradition of the let's-start-today books, shall we begin, *now*, to look at ourselves in an entirely new way – as *receivers*? Shall we start now, to see ourselves in *God's* way, rather than as 'difficult subjects'? It may take a little courage, but let's say about those barriers: 'They may have seemed barriers to me – but they're *not* barriers to Him.'

Here is a prayer which we may like to use:

Dear Lord,
For so long I have seen all those weaknesses
and life-experiences as me. I see that these
intruders can no longer stand in the way of
a wonderful relationship between us – one
which You have always wanted for me.
Right now, I concentrate upon Your love's
influence, *the divine power which is*
beginning to change me – change me from
someone who wistfully tries to believe that
I am a new person (or tries to convince
others that I am). Instead, under Your love's
influence, I am going to be that new person.
Thank You.

Chapter Four

If we peep in, imaginatively, at those encounters which Jesus our Lord had when He walked about on this planet, we'll see the love-influence at work.

And we'll notice something disappearing from those whom Jesus met – their *past*.

People like Zaccheus (away went his greedy past), Mary Magdalene (away went her promiscuous way of life), Bartimeus (an end to his shut-in world) …

Hundreds of ordinary people finding that the love which flowed from Jesus meant the past dropping away like a dead weight.

So much so, that those people reacted joyfully far beyond mere gratitude, didn't they? They knew that something wonderful had happened to them. The past, with its barriers to happiness, had been left behind – for good. The look from Jesus had been more than a look of compassion or under-standing; it had been a look of *power*.

People were *changed* by the influence of love coming from Him – in many cases without specific prayer or word of command.

But surely, some may be thinking, surely we can't all expect the same *instant* changes?

I agree. A book which glibly suggested this, would raise false hopes, wouldn't it?

Yes, of course it's wonderful if we're suddenly set free from the past in dramatic fashion. But what really matters is that there is now to be a very definite *improve-ment* – and this is precisely what con-sciously being in the divine *influence* will bring about. Often more quickly than we dreamt was possible!

When we find God's secret and see His love for us as a decisive influence, change *must* begin.

It can be very helpful to picture God's love-influence as a *light*, powerfully affect-ing every part of us. We can picture Jesus, the *source* of that divine influence, His arms outstretched towards us, *giving to us* …

This powerful love-influence acts in two ways: firstly, upon all that is *in* us, making us tranquil – both about the present and the future; secondly, upon our relationships, and all that involves the world around us.

We now notice how the divine influence brings results where intense effort has failed. We're opening the door to a completely new life. The Saviour of the world, the source of power, is now *central* to us.

Don't worry if *some* situations 'appear' unchanged – for a time at any rate. Just resolutely *thank* the Lord that changes are happening.

Unless we are, perhaps, a weary book-reviewer who may be irritated by repetition, don't see the chapters of this book as needing to be 'got through'. Allow lots of time between the chapters for learning to *recognize* the love-influence at work – recognized as we start each day, and continuing until we sink into that same influence at bedtime.

Lord,

It's exciting to think that for the rest of my
life I can be aware of the active influence
of Your love upon me. Right now, I will
begin to live consciously in the light of
that influence.

I know that as I recognize the power
ontained within Your love, so much will be
changing. As I do so, I will see clearly, at
:st, what really is important; I will see those
disturbing factors in their true proportion.

Thank You again, Lord, for the changes
which You are starting to bring about.

Chapter Five

What is the use of a future if it is merely a continuation of what exists now?

Until now, we may have felt that our past must, inevitably, reach into the future and ruin it, even if we're still quite young!

We may cling, grimly, to Jesus's promise of a bright future after tribulation, but 'realism' keeps intruding: 'Here I am, stuck with this personality and its fears, destined to grow older in a difficult world.'

Resignation to the years ahead for many of us.

But God has let us into His secret! Accepting the power of God's love-influence, the past need *not* mould the future for one day longer.

We know, of course, that there will be challenges. The bodily machine will break down in various ways, the environment may become suddenly frightening, there

vill be loss of loved ones, and heartbreak.
n fact, there will be the strongest tempta-
ion to react to circumstances in the old
vays, forgetting all about the love-influence.
But even in the darkest places light will
come if it has become second nature to live
n that influence. In the darkness, that
nfluence of Jesus will beam down upon us
ınd give us strength *just* to hold on, though
heartbroken at times.

An experiment. Try to think *simultan-
eously* about (a) that uncertain future, with
its potential for great difficulty and (b)
Jesus's love in that future.

How does the future seem as we do this?

Normally, (b) starts to dissolve the
apprehension contained in (a).

What the love-influence of God does, in
fact, is to *light up* the future and *transform*
so much of our natural apprehension.

Obviously, some questions must be asked:
Will we be able to keep our attention upon
the love-influence in the midst of the very
painful daily realities: the failing marriage,

the financial problems, the difficult col-
leagues, the person who won't forgive us?

Certainly, these things could distract us
completely, from focusing upon God's
influence. But do remember that these
experiences must be classified (like all the
other things we have mentioned) as
barriers which *do not exist*, as such, for God
Therefore, we can see these things as
unable to prevent God's influence from
reaching us.

In case anyone thinks that what has
been said is just playing with words, we
have only to look at our Bible to see the
acquired skill, possessed by so many of its
heroes, of managing to be lost in God's love
in the most awful human situations; they
kept within the love-influence, even if they
didn't always think of it, precisely, in this
way!

Just look at some of the familiar hymns
to see the *transforming* of dark circumstance
by those who had learned the same secret.

One of the things which Jesus does so
wonderfully is to assure us that He has
already arrived at those places which cause

us to be afraid, waiting for us with all that we need.

In the influence of Jesus's love, the future *must*, ultimately, be a bright one, because that influence represents *power* over everything which could now make us afraid.

Dear Lord,
For a little while I'm going to sit down and
look at the future! I'm going to see that
future in the light of Your love's powerful
influence upon me.
You are well aware that my human nature
shrinks from future illness or loneliness,
but I know that when I reach those places,
Your influence will still be there, helping me
to be calm and courageous.
Even in the darkest circumstances, I know
that the influence of Your love will mean that
hope can never disappear.
Thank You.

Chapter Six

To use the phrase 'the *light* of God's love-influence' is not just a figure of speech. We really do see things with increased clarity as that light is turned upon the world around us.

The more we are open to the love-influence, the more we can evaluate what is in the complex pattern of events, and of people, of which we're part. We now have a light by which we can see beyond the superficial; we see, instinctively, what can't be trusted, we see that which it would be foolish to follow, that which represents danger. In the same way, we begin to see the sheer goodness in people who may present an exterior which we don't like very much!

And, of course, under the same light, we see more clearly what is in *us*. We will see more readily what is still coming between Jesus and ourselves.

Some of the baffling choices are now dealt with almost instinctively – people of an anxious temperament taking a little longer!

Decisions … Perhaps there's a choice which we know, deep within us, is going to change the direction of our life. Instead of the usual list of 'for and against', with things delicately balanced, we must deliberately let the light of God's love-influence shine upon the problem.

As we learn to look at situations of choice, very aware of the love-influence, there is a growing instinct about the right course. We gain the ability to see the situation through the eyes of Jesus, as His light falls upon it.

We find that it becomes second nature to test the situations into which we move by the light of the love-influence; we develop an alertness in 'interpreting' the signals which the world gives to us.

Under the influence of God's love, our own judgement is starting to blend with His own wisdom.

There's no need to be afraid, once we've made a choice in the light of love's influence. Sometimes the things resulting immediately from the choice will cause us to panic or to have grave misgivings – 'Oh dear, what have I done?' But God does not deceive us; the *long-term* results of choosing by His light are always sure.

By the way, what an improvement there is in relationships when they are the subject of divine enlightenment! We have seen how evil constantly lies to us, how we can become paranoid, and feel that we have to defend ourselves against someone's ill-will towards us. Things which we have 'accepted' in our minds, from evil, can lead to a disastrous intention being formed. 'With Me, you won't be walking in the dark any more,' says Jesus, in that exciting teaching about Him being the light of the world. It's all about His love keeping us on a *safe* path in a confusing world, as we allow its influence.

Dear Lord,
I will remember, as a discipline, to look at
every situation in the light of Your love's
influence. I know that, as You enlighten me,
I will avoid all sorts of things which would
hold up my progress, or be disastrous for
myself – and others.
Thank You.

Chapter Seven

Here's John; it's always a tricky moment when I'm face-to-face with him. John is one of those moody Christians ...

I'm sure that John doesn't feel the slightest warmth towards me, or approval of me. I could dodge this encounter by walking neatly to the right, as if I hadn't seen John; at least I'd be spared my resentment if he responded to my 'hello' with a cold parting of the lips.

But here I am, temporarily forgetting the love-influence!

Remembering the divine influence, I find the courage to look John straight in the eyes, and greet him warmly.

Does John respond? If he doesn't, so what? The love-influence gave me a victory; it dissolved, in advance, my feeling of annoyance if John was as distant as ever. As I focus upon the divine influence, we can't rule out John being 'melted' and responding warmly.

In any event, I'll always say a little prayer for the Lord to bless John, who may have great needs.

One of the obvious aspects of focusing upon the love-influence of Jesus is that of being able to *rise above* previous reactions to the way in which others treat us.

Not being robots, we're going to react with a degree of sensitivity to people around us, but as we learn to *use* the love-influence, it can *envelop* the hurts and then dissolve them.

It's as if Jesus is saying, 'Now, come on. Are you brooding on what that person said to you? Are you brooding on how that other person gossiped about your character? Are you forgetting to think of My love-influence?'

How often we forget to contrast the *impermanence* of the world's circumstances with the ongoing nature of Jesus's love. The great saints always stressed how everything is passing except God. But sadly we often forget this.

As we learn the skill of letting the love-influence dissolve hurts, we realize that we really *have* moved on to a higher plane! The presence of the Source of the love-influence becomes stronger and far more important than the fortunes and mis-fortunes of each day, and we gain a wise detachment about these things. Life's passing experiences are transformed by the *permanent fact* of Jesus, so that His love-influence becomes the *background* against which everything else is seen, wonderfully strengthening our relationship with Him.

St Paul stressed that love goes on for ever. And so, therefore, does its influence!

Lord,
*I let the light of Your love-influence shine
upon those painful areas which are due to
other people's imperfections and to my own.
I think of those things now, slowly, one by
one; I think of the people with whom there
may exist a state of disharmony. I allow
the influence of Your love to dissolve
all resentment.*
*The power of Your love is helping me to see
things in their true proportions at last;
I see Your love making these disturbances
powerless to affect the upwards direction
of my walk with You.*
Thank You.

Chapter Eight

We would all like to be free – from something, or, perhaps, from someone!

I have to smile, when listening to some of the 'pop' songs, at how often we get the phrase 'Set me free' – or, as one unfortunate romantic partner was told: 'Get out of my life!'

If we could eliminate every troublesome relationship from our life we would still want to be free from things *within* us, wouldn't we? Many people who fiercely claim to be free and independent (especially of those oppressive religious beliefs!) are shaped by their environment much more than they realize.

Of all the things from which people would like to be free, I'm sure that fear would be near the top of the list. About fear, we must remember that Jesus once said, 'If I set you free, you really are free!'

What a promise! We soon find that one most important aspect of the love-influence is that it is *liberating*.

Fear is typical of the human problems upon which the influence of Jesus has a transforming effect, succeeding where 'positive-thinking' methods fail. When Jesus begins to set us free, it opens the way for a heightened experience of life's many good things, which fear (in one form or another) usually manages to spoil.

When the power contained in the love-influence loosens some of the chains from the past, it's as if we can begin to be a little more adventurous. We're given permission to live!

I mentioned fear because it is the favourite weapon of those supernatural evil forces which oppose God's loving plans for us. (I haven't referred to those evil forces so far, but can assure any sceptical person that it's *not* old-fashioned to take these forces seriously. Jesus did – and does!)

Fear drives us into chaotic situations, into hatreds, into assassinations, into world wars, and into self-destruction. Fear makes is morbidly concerned about what people think of us, it warps our judgements and it freezes the love which we could feel for people.

Our various fears *do* diminish as we very deliberately open ourselves up to the influence of Jesus's love. This I can promise.

Most of us are aware of another sinister area which is tangled up with fear – that is, of course, the self-condemning part of us. I am not talking about the healthy disgust with ourselves when we have behaved badly. I mean the nagging 'neurotic' guilt which so often persists even when we have asked God for forgiveness, and honestly believe that we have received it.

Again, nagging guilt can be a favourite weapon of evil forces; if evil can make us accept the lie that we don't deserve forgiveness, then we may become permanently self-condemned. It is vital to use the love-influence to wear down these areas of guilt. We must be very bold when receiving the Lord's forgiveness. We must look into the light of His love and say: 'Thank You, Lord. I have *nothing* for which to condemn or to punish myself.' We need to do this every time, so that it really sinks down. We need to say it very defiantly to evil too: 'The Lord has forgiven me. There is nothing for which to condemn or to punish myself.'

Those greatly used by God soon find that evil is both subtle and powerful. We must, therefore, keep firmly in mind that the love-influence is a *power*, a power greater than those opposing forces, a power possessed only by the Creator of the universe.

The roots of fear and self-condemnation may lie very deep but they *are* loosened by that power as we surrender to it. Love setting us free.

Lord,
I believe that unless it comes from You,
freedom is partial and temporary. With all
my heart I accept Your promise of freedom.
I realize that the influence of Your love is
a liberating influence.
Thank You.

Chapter Nine

A very short chapter, just to remind us that, as Jesus sets us free, it is in order to take us somewhere else!

Remember, always, those outstretched hands. Jesus does not set us free to live in a vacuum, but in order to make sure that we are *lifted* into His Kingdom of love – permanently.

Yes, Jesus has a great longing. From our birth He longs to draw us into Himself, into eventual oneness. If we live in the love-influence, that is precisely what is happening.

We must be quite clear that we're not being brought into a comfortable trouble-free existence, escaping from earth's more painful places; that is not promised to us. But the road upon which the love-influence shines (though not trouble-free) is the only truly safe road.

Although we have to live to the world's timetable, to a large extent, we can look into that love-influence and be immersed in *another* dimension within seconds. All this can be combined with the simplest whisper of a phrase such as 'In Your love.'

Just as times of prayer and Bible-reading are crucial, so are those *recollections* of His love-influence which always mean that the ever-present Lord Jesus lifts up our thoughts to where they belong!

Dear Lord,
Help me to see Your influence each day as
my true and permanent environment.
Thank You.

Chapter Ten

Already, many will have noticed a very important aspect of the divine love-influence – its power to heal.

Initially the influence would have been a *cleansing* one – the light of God burning up all sorts of wrong ways of thinking. Cynicism, intolerance, grudges, begin to feel increasingly uncomfortable guests in us, and prepare to leave.

We find ourselves taking sides with God against things in us which we had tolerated – sometimes almost affectionately! It is all part of healing.

Without even asking, specifically, for healing in a particular area, the consciousness of the divine influence is, *in itself*, a healing consciousness.

We need to be quite specific about what is happening as the love-influence reaches us, and deliberately to thank God or it – 'Thank You, Lord, for the healing of Your love'. This is no make-believe process, no mere 'self-conditioning' regime, but simply *allowing* the power of the Creator to work. The healing of God's love-influence is especially true in the sphere of the emotions. Emotional healing, of course, can so often affect, beneficially, the physical.

I do realize that many have been to healing services, had hands laid on them, perhaps, but are not conscious of 'being healed'. Many are tempted to abandon their faith. For anyone in this category I would say, 'Don't stop fully opening yourself up to the love-influence every day – even after many disappointments about specific requests.' This influence just cannot help *in some way* bringing about good results, even if, for the moment, it isn't the specific need upper-most in our minds.

Many things promise to 'renew' us; some of them do for a time, but are limited. The love-influence of Jesus, however, is the one miraculous *renewing force*, making new the essential you and me – the spirit, which is so dear to God.

Almost every writer on healing today will tell us that it is a subject far wider and more intricate than we could imagine. But we can be very sure always of the *healing* nature of Jesus's love. There's no true healing *outside* it.

We can, therefore, thank Him for all that is within us which His love's influence is healing, from the very moment that we opened ourselves up to it.

Dear Lord,
As Your love-influence reaches me,
thank You that so many aspects of my
existence are being renewed. Thank You that
physically, emotionally and spiritually, there
is, every day, a healing process. I shall go on
looking towards You, and away from
all those limitations!
Thank You.

Chapter Eleven

By this time we may be picturing, instinctively, the outstretched hands of Jesus, as His love-influence reaches us. One aspect of this reaching out is His supply.

Love *guarantees* supply. Nothing which Jesus sees as good for us now, or in the future, will ever be held back from us. The supply will be there for us precisely when needed – not before it is needed, and not, of course, when it's too late.

Those who have allowed Jesus to become their friend soon notice His *anticipation*. We ourselves can show anticipatory love to one another, but we only see its *perfection* in the way in which Jesus our Lord deals with us. If we allow His love's *influence*, Jesus is able to exercise this anticipatory supply in wonderful ways. We find needs met in a way which shows that He has been at work before we reached the need-situation.

The supply which comes from Jesus is without imperfection and is very much part of the love-influence; all it needs is our *recognition*. This is why anticipatory thanks are such a good idea: 'Lord, I don't quite see how I'm going to struggle through that occasion, but thank You that You *will* give me what I need.' 'Lord, it's beyond me to see how the bills will be paid, but thank You that You *won't* let me down,' and so on.

We find that the divine provision is by no means restricted to our material needs. The supply always comes in the form of very specific intervention – courage given at that interview, patience given in a demanding relationship, love given when nursing a sick person. Under love's influence, the spirit's needs are met in a way which the world can't possibly meet them. Jesus's awareness of our needs accounts for the many instances of the uncanny finding of lost articles when we've stopped looking frantically and prayed instead!

As living within the love-influence becomes second-nature, we can *know* that our spiritual, mental and material needs are

being met. It all comes down to *recognition*.
Recognition and thanks – both for the
love-influence, and for the supply which
always comes with it.

Lord,
Help me to develop the awareness of felt
needs being met by Your unfailing supply.
Even when I don't recognize a need,
or when I forget to call on You, I know
that Your supply will be there for me.
Thank You.

Chapter Twelve

Let us keep that picture of Jesus reaching out to us for a few moments. Not only is He meeting needs, but reaching out to put something of His own nature into us. Yes, the love-influence means *absorbing* what He is.

Already, because God made us in His own likeness, there are reflections, in us, of the divine qualities. Sadly, as we know, these reflections can become obscured. Jesus wants to reach into us and develop those divine qualities which we'll need for eternity!

Therefore, when we look up into that love-influence, it's really a look of agreement with all that He wants to do in us. We're giving our consent to the life of Jesus *expanding* in us.

We soon learn that our own efforts to shape our character are not enough.

As St Paul found, it just has to be *God's work* – producing what mere attempts at self-improvement could never achieve.

It's quite possible for that rather apologetic person with a poor self-image to be a victorious person in the things which really matter. As we absorb the divine influence, we are bound to be winning all sorts of victories – not always recognized at the time.

The qualities we have *absorbed* start to be available for other people. This is the often-forgotten way (more than words) which draws others to Him.

Just think of what we're absorbing! Or, better still, *who* we're absorbing.

The usual warning has to be given, of course. We don't peer anxiously to see if we're becoming reflections of Jesus! We simply *allow* the absorption-process and keep our gaze upon the Source.

I realize that the concept of Jesus at work in us, making us more like Himself, is hardly original! But what may be new for

many of us – and decisive – is discovering
the wonderful interior-changes which come
from living, *consciously*, within that
influence.

Lord,
I need to be much more like You in order to
negotiate this present existence victoriously.
Let my look into Your constant influence of
love be my consent to Your work in me,
as I absorb Your qualities.
Thank You.

Chapter Thirteen

Jesus expanding His influence, not only in us, but *through* us …

'Serving God.' Oh dear, this is so often represented as an uphill occupation – something which we may need to force ourselves to do, bringing just occasional satisfaction.

There is a far better way of looking at what we do for God. As we focus upon the love-influence, it means that we're living in the *light*; we then realize that we have an opportunity to let other people live in that same light! We're now in the best possible state to *respond* to the world and its needs.

Here is Mary, who seems to be in a shocking state when we bump into her. We don't need to think of our 'serving' or 'helping' Mary. Better to picture the light of the divine love-influence shining on both of us, and then let our conversation take place *within that light.*

Of course, we wouldn't embarrass Mary by telling her that we were both within the love-influence of Jesus at that moment! But, for our part, we would listen to what Mary has to say, firmly believing that His light, His influence, is all around us, as He gives us the right words.

Visualizing Jesus's love-influence is very *relaxing* when encountering others. It goes far beyond playing at make-believe and making nice, mental, 'spiritual' pictures; the Lord Jesus is *right there* – guiding our conversation, prompting us about what we might do for someone. Although she may not realize it, Mary is a receiver of that powerful divine influence; she is sharing it with us at that moment, and it's the beginning of her need being met, if she is willing.

If we're learning the art of resting, con-sciously, in the love-influence when with others, this is the best possible condition for His power to flow. No need for a contrived setting, such as a praise-filled

Christian convention, but simply letting the influence of love take over in that quiet one-to-one contact.

As we 'carry' the love-influence around with us, we must value *every* meeting we have – refusing impatience if a person is not the one we were hoping to see! *In some way* Jesus will be reaching out from us, even in the most casual-seeming or 'unresponsive' encounter.

To mention Mary yet again, the love-influence will be breaking down barriers in *her*. And if we find ourselves offering to pray with Mary, we can be absolutely sure that there, in the love-influence, a power to heal and uplift her is being released.

Normally, we can never be sure whether our 'words of wisdom' or attempts at persuasion are hitting any target. If we're forgetting the presence of Jesus, they could well be wasted efforts! If, however, we consciously keep within that influence of power, then everything occurring will have a *lasting* quality about it.

If we keep in the light of the love-influence I firmly believe that we are *projecting* it to those for whom we pray (as a *fact*, not just something within our own mind). Our prayer will be Spirit-led and there will be that wonderful assurance that someone is receiving, according to the need which God sees.

The process is completed by the word of thanks to our Lord, that either the prayer we said, or the contact we made, is *being used*, beyond any doubt.

As we realize that God's love is not merely an attitude towards us, but a powerful influence, we find one area of life after another being affected, including that of our sharing Him with others. God's Kingdom is one of light, and we're now helping to make it more widespread.

Dear Lord,
I will remember each day that, wherever I
go, there is the influence of Your love. I will
remember to see its light enfolding not only
myself, but those whom I meet.
I thank You, now, for all the good which will
come from those encounters with others.

Chapter Fourteen

What about the unexpected crises, when we wonder how on earth we can possibly come through, when we doubt our ability to deal with what has suddenly turned our life upside down?

Can the surrounding influence of the divine love make a difference?

Can it make a difference, even when we've had the thought of not wanting to go on living?

We wouldn't be human if life's tragedies *didn't* have the power to shatter us. We only have to remember what happened when our Lord was called to the tomb of his friend, Lazarus. He did not 'react positively' or with detachment. He *cried*, didn't He?

One aspect of the vast subject of human suffering, which cannot be examined in depth here, is that the forces of evil work to exploit, and make much worse, the things which happen to us. It is because of this exploitation that we must, if we possibly can, allow the divine love to enter *immediately* that which has overwhelmed us. If we can do this, though still in a state of shock, terrible shock, we can be sure that Jesus's love now *stands guard* against those forces which would worsen the situation. All that we may be able to say with broken voice is 'Lord, I trust Your love,' (even though the darkness ahead seems unrelieved).

As we make this almost helpless surrender to His love's influence upon our situation we may catch His whisper into our heart: 'My child, as I share this with you, let the power of My *love* help you to bear it.'

As we find just a little courage (very fragile) we realize that the influence of our Lord's love is mysteriously saving us from being *completely* broken.

Dear Lord,
I believe that You are able to share the
darkest places – those major *situations of*
fear which I feel I could never face, as I let
Your love's influence enfold me.

Chapter Fifteen

Living consciously within Jesus's love-influence is all about *contrasts*. Instead of those half-convinced, half-convincing statements about being a new person as a Christian, we now find that life in His love really does contrast sharply with life previously.

We can now confront the sort of daily situations in which we were usually defeated, and, in the light of His love, re-enter those areas victoriously.

Surrounded by His light, we face the circumstances with a power which we never dreamt we possessed.

We can reflect: 'Just to think that I could have been victorious in this sort of thing all along – instead of having those crushing failures.'

The love-influence will produce contrasts such as these, if we really *surrender* ourselves to it :

> Indecision giving way to boldness,
> Agitation giving way to serenity,
> Weakness giving way to courage,
> Cynicism giving way to tolerance,
> Self-concern giving way to out-going love,
> Impulsiveness giving way to patience,
> Persistent anxiety giving way to quiet joy.

Keeping aware of Jesus's influence, we're also going to *recognize* those important *turning-points* – times when our choices will have a long-term significance. In His light we will choose with wisdom and see through any deception by forces opposed to God. The divine influence will be keeping out all that would confuse our mental processes; we will stop brooding upon hurts, or supposed hurts, and be able to pray for those 'troublesome' people – *really* wishing good to come to them. Contrasts at last!

Now, just a word to any who may feel that picturing the love-influence is a little unreal or stretching our imagination too far.

Many times during a day, in order to keep up his or her spirits, a person may 'picture' a beloved relative or friend. If we believe that God is just as real as that loved one or friend, then it makes sense to think much about His love!

Seeing the *light* of that influence is much more than a merely subjective vision, because wherever Jesus is, there *is* light; evil forces, which we may never have dreamt existed, can't operate in that light. This light is often seen as a wall of fire around Christians in countries where naked evil is practised.

Let us remember, too, that as we turn to the light of Jesus's love, it meets *His* longing in a world which, on the whole, doesn't make much room for Him.

There is so much that could be written about that event two thousand years ago when God stepped into our world. What we see, linking everything together, of course, is love …

As millions have done, we can look at the Cross and see *love* surrendering all, *love* taking the world's guilt-burden, *love* triumphant when all seemed lost. It is *this* love, seen on the Cross, which continues its victorious work. If we say 'yes' to its influence upon us, we will experience just how powerful is that love.

In this terribly unpredictable existence, the influence of Jesus's love is there to steady us, and we're no longer at the mercy of the rapidly changing fortunes of each day. We acquire the *skill* of avoiding things which we used to allow far too easily – simply because they were not illuminated!

Dear Lord,
Within the influence of Your love I can now
act upon Your promise about making all
things new. I will prove that new life in my
changed reactions, because the power of
Your influence will be there at every
moment, for me to draw upon – producing
contrasts with my past.

Chapter Sixteen

The most realistic way to see our future is to see it *filled* with Jesus. We must grasp God's *eagerness* for us to enjoy what He has been getting ready for us. The many promises of God are simply expressions of the love in which we now consciously live. If we look to love's brightness those promises will light up, too!

❧

The walk within the love-influence is an upwards walk, and in a new direction. If we grasp Jesus by the hand, so to speak, He is lifting us forward – we will be *lifted through* those dark periods which may lie ahead.

As we remain in the influence of His love, Jesus our Lord will be removing all sorts of obstacles; these will include obstacles which we didn't pray about because we weren't aware of their existence! Jesus is our navigator. Keeping within His influence, we can be sure that He is excluding all that would be bad for our inheritance. He will be making harmony of our circumstances. We need not run away from what lies ahead of us, because His light already shines on the road we've taken. The light says to us: 'Forget the past; the look is forward.'

As we become 'lost' in the love-influence shining upon our road, we realize that, eventually, there can only be *better* things in store for us – joys which will be permanent. Jesus becomes the *hope* of whatever particular existence is ours, *expertly* fitting the details into His plan for us; no evil forces will be able to frustrate that plan. Our destiny is *perfection* and not one step towards it will be taken alone. That perfection will be, essentially, all about love. *Our* growing love will *blend* with that divine love into which we look every day.

Obviously, within the light of Jesus's love, we won't be able to ignore the world's darkness – but we're going to see the light overcome the darkness. As we keep focused upon Jesus, we will learn to see His love as the *background* to all phenomena; we will see every problem against that background; we will see that all God's ways (including His justice) are, in fact, love-inspired.

The ever-growing sense of Jesus's love will draw out our *worship* of Him. Expressions such as 'dearest Lord', 'wonderful Lord' (which once seemed reserved for a spiritual elite, and well beyond us!) will now be spontaneous. Within the influence of His love we will find ourselves telling the Lord, gently, how much we love Him – in fact, just naturally having His name, frequently, on our lips. And we will often give Him that *submissive* look ('Whatever *You* wish, Lord').

Looking into the light of Jesus's love we'll be aware of a growing *closeness* which we can begin to *use*. We will very much have the sense of our walk being shared; we will *know* that we're loved even when, perhaps, human loves are missing. The influence coming from Jesus will be exerted to *keep* us on the road chosen for us. No longer will we think of heaven and earth as separate states, because our life here will have that definite heavenly dimension.

When events in our existence puzzle us from time to time, we'll remember God's knowledge of our future, and His certain influence in it; we will then be content to let Him work out His plans! If we allow it, the light of the love-influence will now burn steadily for us right through to the end of our life; it will be shining *in* us and *around* us, helping us to endure all that life can produce.

Where is the divine love-influence taking us? It is taking us to the place where love is *everything*.

As St Paul might have said in his famous letter to the Christians at Corinth: 'Love's *influence* achieves all things.'

Dear Lord,
Please make this a turning point.
May there be a different quality of life
as I surrender to the influence of Your
love – whatever the circumstances.
I know that I will see those
circumstances transformed.
Thank You.

Other books from John Woolley

I AM WITH YOU

Since 1984 people throughout the world have been discovering the power to change lives of the little devotional book, *I Am With You*.

The divinely inspired words bring a sense of our Lord's presence, in a wonderful way, to strengthen the reader in his or her personal need.

I commend this little book to all who are seeking to deepen their spiritual lives.
– Cardinal Basil Hume, England

I Am With You *is a very special book; it will bless countless people.*
– Prebendary John Pearce, England

I have never experienced such a closeness to Jesus.
– Fran Gunning, USA

A lovely book of devotions; we use it daily.
– Dr Donald English,
former President, Methodist Conference

I Am With You *will deeply touch many people.*
– Fr. Robert de Grandis, USA

The most wonderful book I have ever read.
– Fr. Tom Cass, England

SORROW INTO JOY

Since the publication of the well-loved devotional classic, *I Am With You*, further words from the risen Lord Jesus Christ have been received by Fr. John in times of prayer.

Sorrow Into Joy takes us into the mystery of the suffering which so many endure today. We look anew at the power of the Cross, and at the love which still shines in the world's darkness.

Our Lord's words give us courage, as we glimpse the eternity when all things will be made new.

PRAYERS FOR THE FAMILY

There is a very familiar saying that 'families which pray together, stay together.'

If, from the earliest days, older and younger can share prayer-times, they become aware of God's provision and protection for that family in a very special way; they become sure that He is interested in every detail of that family's existence.

Using these prayers, boys and girls can progress from saying them with their parents, or older relatives, into making up their own prayers. It is not long before the young ones enjoy the daily habit of talking with Jesus on their own.

THE FRIENDSHIP OF JESUS

Already this book has helped many (of all ages)
to find life's one vital friendship.

The book was written, firstly, for those with
little or no faith, and secondly for 'believers'
wanting to experience Jesus more warmly. As
we follow the very simple steps, God will be at
work to bring about a *lasting* friendship.

The Friendship of Jesus is extremely helpful.
I doubt if anyone could fail to profit
from reading it.
– Dr Stuart Blanch,
former Archbishop of York

This lovely book.
– Canadian reader

This book is both very beautiful and very
practical
– a rare combination. It gives us new insights
whenever it is read or re-read.
What a friend we have in Jesus!
– London reader

I have seen lives wonderfully changed
by this little book.
– Church leader, South of England

I just couldn't put the book down.
– Asian immigrant,
becoming a Christian

WORDS OF POWER

Searching through the Bible, we find many verses in which God speaks to us directly – words with a particular power to change our situations. These heart-to-heart verses provide us with a wonderful way of receiving our Lord's own Person, lifting us out of fear or discouragement or confusion.

This collection of 'direct quotes' covers many themes – forgiveness, temptation, healing, the future, an awareness of God's love. Each theme has its own suggested prayers to help us build these words into our daily experience.

The result of absorbing these words of power each day is an increasing sense of God indwelling us, and an awareness that, in meeting life's inevitable challenges, we're not alone.